THE JUDAISM AND MODERN TIMES
SERIES

ON THE WAY TO A
JEWISH STATE

ISRAEL POLITICS ACCORDING TO
KABBALAH

RABBI YITZCHAK GINSBURGH

GAL EINAI
JERUSALEM • NEW YORK

ON THE WAY TO A JEWISH STATE: Israel Politics According to
Kabbalah

By Rabbi Yitzchak Ginsburgh

Printed in the United States of America and Israel
First Edition

For information:
Israel: GAL EINAI
PO Box 1015
Kfar Chabad 72915
tel. (in Israel): 1-700-700-966
tel. (from abroad): 972-3-9608008
Email: books@inner.org
Web: www.inner.org

GAL EINAI produces and publishes books, pamphlets, audiocas-
settes and videocassettes by Rabbi Yitzchak Ginsburgh. To receive
a catalog of our products in English and/or Hebrew, please con-
tact us at any of the above addresses, email orders@inner.org or
call our orders department in Israel.

ISBN: 978-965-7146-84-2

Book Layout ©2013 BookDesignTemplates.com

"נכון שיכתוב בצורת ספר השיעורים שלומד.
בברכה להצלחה"

"…It would be proper to publish your classes in book form.
With blessings for success…"

— *from a letter from the Lubavitcher Rebbe
to the author, Elul 5741*

THE TEACHINGS OF KABBALAH SERIES

By Rabbi Yitzchak Ginsburgh
(in English)

The Hebrew Letters: Channels of Creative Consciousness

The Mystery of Marriage: How to Find True Love and Happiness in Married Life

Awakening the Spark Within: Five Dynamics of Leadership that can Change the World

Transforming Darkness into Light: Kabbalah and Psychology

Rectifying the State of Israel: A Political Platform based on Kabbalah

Living in Divine Space: Kabbalah and Meditation

Body, Mind, and Soul: Kabbalah on Human Physiology, Disease, and Healing

Consciousness & Choice: Finding Your Soulmate

The Art of Education: Internalizing Ever-New Horizons

What You Need to Know About Kabbalah

Kabbalah and Meditation for the Nations

Anatomy of the Soul

A Sense of the Supernatural: Interpretation of Dreams and Paranormal Experiences

Lectures on Torah and Modern Physics

CONTENTS

Preface

The phrase, "A Jewish state in the Land of Israel" plucks at the deepest heartstrings of every yearning Jew. For generations, since the destruction of the Temple and the exile to the diaspora, we have believed and hoped, prayed and dreamed about the ingathering of the exiles and our return to living in our Land standing tall, asking God to "break the yoke of the nations from over our necks and lead us to our land standing tall."[1] The ultimate goal of our yearning is the complete redemption, the arrival of Mashiach and the construction of the Temple. There is no doubt that a Jewish state is an essential and central component of the grand picture of the redemption of the Jewish People.

Yet, it is clear that the state that was established on 5th Iyar 5708 (1948), as it stands today, is still a far cry from that dreamlike vision that has warmed our hearts for almost two thousand years. It is not difficult to understand why many Torah and mitzvah observant Jews are reluctant to identify themselves with the state and its symbols. Attesting to this problem are the festivities of Yom Ha'atzmaut, around which rages a long and intense controversy within the religious community in Israel.

One might suppose that the differences of opinions will not end in the near future. However, we can and must arise above them and join together when it comes to the main issue, which is: **what type of state do we want and what are we doing to achieve it?** This is a constructive and positive activity that not only relates to what has been and what currently exists, but mainly turns its face to the future with the goal of rectifying and healing reality.

Notes

[1] From the *ahavat olam* blessing recited before the *kriyat shema* every morning.

Introduction to the Platform

One might suppose that the differences of opinions will not end in the near future. However, we can and must rise above them and unite regarding the main issue, which is: **what type of state do we want and what are we doing to achieve it?** This is a constructive and positive activity that relates to the future with the goal of rectifying and healing reality, instead of harping incessantly on the past and present situations. This vision should be so inviting and pleasant that every Jewish individual will readily want to identify with it, culminating in a critical mass of change – the "tipping point" – when a broad spectrum of the public will be active in actualizing the vision.

But before we present our "platform" for rectifying the state, it is important to stress that the order should not be perceived as inflexible – like a binding mathematical sequence – but as an initial suggestion within which there is a lot of room for flexibility. In practice, we need to turn a sensitive ear to what happens in reality – as in the Kabbalistic concept of "returning light" – seeing what needs to be done

3

and how best to act at every given moment. This is because reality is dynamic, and just as our psyche does not necessarily work "according to the book," and will never be a programmed computer, so too real life is constantly developing and changing. Thus a large measure of sensitivity is needed to determine how to act within it and how to elevate it.[1]

Notes

[1] For instance, as Maimonides states (Laws of Kings 12:2), "All of these things and their like no one will ever know how they will be until they happen."

[1]

Step One: Spiritual Motivation – the Crown

Rectifying the state of Israel begins from the "above ground" *sefirah* of *keter* (crown). It is from here that the rest of the system flows. Like a crown that is placed on top of the head, this *sefirah* represents the level of super-conscious experience in the soul. Within the crown are the three levels of faith, pleasure, and will.

The first thing that is needed to change a situation is faith, specifically the faith which begins with belief in God, the Creator, who does only good, and concludes with faith in the pleasant future that awaits us, "I believe with perfect faith that Mashiach will arrive."[1]

After the level of faith comes pleasure where abstract faith begins to be integrated as an initial experience of pure, simple pleasure that revives the soul. Here, even faith in the coming of Mashiach is no longer something ethereal and vague, but manifests as a motivating power, which we can tap into by in-depth study of those Torah issues that relate to redemption.

From the power of pleasure, willpower is born; that resolute power without which nothing could ever be achieved. This is not just a type of faith that hovers above the limitations of time, nor is it just delighting in the promised picture of the future, but is an active drive, to get up and do something, in the knowledge that "nothing stands in the way of willpower." With willpower one can overcome obstacles using strategies that descend to the finest details on the way to a Jewish state without forgetting the ultimate goal.

Notes

[1] The penultimate principle of the Thirteen Principles of Faith according to Maimonides.

Step Two: Torah Authority – Wisdom

Once the foundations of faith have been laid, we reach the level of revealed consciousness. The first of the conscious powers of the human soul is in the *sefirah* of *chochmah* (wisdom), "The beginning is wisdom."[1] Wisdom is not yet intellectual perception itself, but like an initial spark; an undeniable experience of seeing the light of truth.

In the context of rectifying the state, wisdom means recognizing that the Torah's authority is above all other authority because the Torah is a "Torah of truth," and there is only one truth. Obviously, the Torah itself grants broad authority to social norms and to the laws of the country, as the sages teach us, "The law of kingdom is law."[2] However, this includes the consideration of our "moral compass" that indicates a hierarchy in which Torah law stands above manmade laws. This comes to the fore in particular in the law that states that whenever there is a contradiction between the mitzvot of the Torah and the king's decree (even a Jewish king who was anointed by a prophet), the Torah's law takes preference.[3]

It might seem that we can give up on this stage prima facie, because, unfortunately, there are many Jewish people today who do not see the Torah as the ultimate source of authority. However, the greatest rule of this rectification process is that "nothing is ever lost."[4] Just as we believe in the Torah, so too we believe in the Jewish People as a whole and we trust that sooner or later the *teshuvah* process will escalate until the grand majority of the nation will lovingly accept the Torah's authority. In order to do so, the current threatening representation of "a state run by Torah law" must be refuted, showing instead how "the State of Torah" is the most beautiful and suitable thing for us as a people.

In the first stages, it will be necessary for those Jews who recognize the Torah, at least, to express this recognition by setting a correct order of priorities in which the Torah takes the place as the ultimate and definitive authority.

Notes

[1] Psalms 111:10.
[2] Maimonides, Laws of Theft and Lost Property, 5:11.
[3] Maimonides, Laws of Kings 3:9.
[4] See *Hayom Yom*, 14th Iyar.

[3]

Step Three: The Consciousness of Wholeness – Understanding

In the human psyche, the *sefirah* of *binah* (understanding) is the stage at which the light of wisdom is integrated and becomes tangible as an integral, well-defined intellectual perception. In the current context, we will place the consciousness of wholeness at this stage of recognition – the wholeness of the Torah, the wholeness of the people and the wholeness of the land.

The wholeness of the Torah means that the Torah must be related to as a composite entity in which each facet contains holiness, yet only when the entire Torah is perceived as one all-inclusive unit can it be correctly illuminated. When "God's Torah is complete, it revives the soul."[1]

The wholeness of the Jewish People comes to the fore in the statement that "All Jews are responsible for one another,"[2] and every Jew has an integral part of the complete picture. This is also the root of the correct attitude towards conversion, as we shine our approval to those righteous converts who join the Jewish People, while taking care not to accept false conversions, which accelerates the dangerous process of inter-marriage that jeopardizes the wholeness of the nation.

The wholeness of the Land of Israel is the simple realization that the entire Holy Land was given to the entire Jewish People by God, the Creator. This fundamental right holds even when the Jewish People is situated on foreign land and is even truer now that we have returned to our land, settled and reclaimed it from foreign hands through extraordinary Divine Providence (for instance, the War of Independence and the Six Day War, which we recall during the month of Iyar).

Notes

[1] Psalms 19:8.
[2] *Sanhedrin* 27b.

[4]

Step Four: "You Have Chosen Us" – Knowledge

After wisdom and understanding comes knowledge. The *sefirah* of *da'at* (knowledge) is not a purely rational power, but a power of the soul that activates intellectual awareness and brings it to the fore in the emotional powers of the soul. Concepts such as recognition and responsibility, free-choice and devotion to a cause, all these belong in particular to the *sefirah* of knowledge, and the Zohar defines knowledge as the "key" that opens the six attributes of the heart.

With reference to rectifying the state of Israel, the *sefirah* of knowledge focuses on the recognition that we are the Chosen People, as the verse states, "And you shall be for Me a treasure from out of all the other nations."[1]

Nowadays, the term "Chosen People" may seem somewhat objectionable, because it is mistakenly identified with racism. This aversion intensifies on the background of the monstrous racist theory (which we will not mention by name), whose proponents brought upon us the darkest,

11

bloodiest period in Jewish history. But, it must be made clear that we are speaking of the difference between light and dark, and the truth is that God's choice of the Jewish People obligates us to a greater responsibility to improve, and includes within it good and blessing for the entire world.

Trying to run away from the uniqueness of the Jewish People, or attempting to create an imaginary equality between everyone is like someone who runs away from his own self and forgets his name and identity. Forgetting one's identity is liable to deteriorate even further to blur the boundaries between friend and foe (which unfortunately happens quite often). So, rectification must be achieved by accepting a correct, deep understanding of our Jewish uniqueness, and by linking to our chain of Jewish tradition through which runs the scarlet thread of recognition that "You have chosen us from all the nations, You love us and have desired us."[2]

So far, we have laid the initial foundation for rectifying the state at both the super-conscious and rational-conscious levels of the soul. Once this correct perception has been achieved, we can begin to descend to the practical levels of the process, like in our human soul from which our emotions and actions stem from the intellect that is above them and motivates them to manifest.

In the first section of this booklet, we laid the initial foundation for rectifying the state of Israel at the super-conscious and conscious-intellect levels of the psyche. With this in mind, we can now turn to the practical implications of the program for building a Jewish state.

Notes

1 Exodus 19:5.
2 From the verses of the kiddush said on festivals.

[5]

Step Five: Settling the Land – Loving-kindness

The first of the attributes of the heart according to Kabbalah is the *sefirah* of *chesed* (loving-kindness). Like the right hand that offers and distributes goodness and blessing to all, this attribute is likewise motivated by love. The archetypal personality for this property is the first Jew, Abraham, the great believer and the man of loving-kindness, as the Torah phrase states, "Loving-kindness is to Abraham."[1]

On the public arena, the main relationship of the Jewish People to the Land of Israel is love, "The greatest sages would kiss the borders of the Land of Israel and kiss its stones and roll in its dust, as it says, 'For Your servants desire its stones and its dust they have favored'[2]."[3] Like a groom who loves his bride, such love effects a powerful attractive force, which, like a magnet, surpasses vast expanses of time and space.

That same love by power of which we have returned to the Land (not just because we were looking for a "safe refuge") must be confirmed by a formal consummation of love, by declaring Jewish sovereignty over the entire country, as a natural right. We must also emphasize that this love is not just a natural love for our homeland, but a love that contains the full array of loving God ("Love *Havayah*, your God"[4]); loving the Jewish People ("'Love your fellowman as you love yourself' is a great rule of the Torah"[5]); and loving the Torah, because this fundamental triplet can only manifest in its entirety in the Land of Israel.

A clear statement must be issued to assert the fact that the source of our right to the Land of Israel is God's promise to us in the Torah (as millions of gentiles all over the world also believe), and that the success of the reestablishment of the Jewish People in its land is only through God's help. The Torah warns us that once we have settled the Land of Israel we should not say, "My power and the might of my hand has made me successful," rather, we should "remember that *Havayah* your God is the one who has given you the power to be successful."[6] Following these lines, we suggest revising the declaration of independence for the Jewish state to include these basic principles of the Jewish People as it returns to its land.

Declaring sovereignty over all parts of the country that are in our possession is the "best thing" that can happen to the Jews and a necessary reaction on our part to the revelation of Divine loving-kindness in our era. This is not referring to a political declaration that is empty of content, but a statement that is accompanied by actions – because actions speak louder than words, as the *mishnah* states, "Say a little and do a lot."[7] We should wholeheartedly support settling the entire country, redeeming land, and developing agriculture and sources of livelihood, while heading towards financial independence and instilling a culture that balks at chasing after luxuries and advocates living modestly and frugally, "Who is rich? One who is happy with their lot,"[8]

"When you eat the efforts of your hand, happy are you and it is good for you."[9] A special emphasis should be placed on encouraging and preferring Jewish labor and raising the prestige of the Jewish worker through brotherly love, as the verse states, "And your brother shall live with you."[10]

Notes

[1] Micah 7:2.
[2] Psalms 102:15.
[3] Maimonides, Laws of Kings 5:10.
[4] Deuteronomy 6:5.
[5] Leviticus 19:18; Rashi ad loc.
[6] Deuteronomy 8:17-18.
[7] *Avot* 1:14.
[8] Ibid 4:1.
[9] Psalms 128:2.
[10] Leviticus 25:36.

[6]

Step Six: Israel's Firm Arm – Might

From the *sefirah* of *chesed* (loving-kindness), we reach the *sefirah* of *gevurah* (might), which stems from the inner sense of fear, the special attribute of Isaac, "Fear of Isaac."[1] Might balances the *sefirah* of loving-kindness, controlling it and guarding its borders, "The left hand pushes away while the right hand draws near"[2]; like the two opposite and complementary poles of a magnet.

Regarding the rectification of the state, might comes to the fore in the concept in Jewish law referred to as, "Israel's firm arm."[3] Military power is not an objective in its own right, and the Jewish Prophets were the ones who gifted the world with a vision of peace, "And they shall pound their swords into spades."[4] Nonetheless, after so many generations under foreign rule, God has returned our power to use political and military force against our enemies (if we would only wish to do so). Might stems from loving-kindness. Out of our love of the Jewish People and our love of the land, we summon the courage to fight the enemy, without any mistaken illusions of achieving peace through surrender. Here are some of the basic guidelines for a correct defense policy according to the Torah:

Firstly, let's not be afraid of our own shadow. Excessive fear stems from a lack of faith and trust in God, as expressed in the phrase, "Fear in Zion, o' sinners."[5] Before he passed away, the Ba'al Shem Tov's elderly father told his young son, "Love every Jew and don't fear anyone or anything other than God Himself." Just as this last testament should be the basis of every Jewish child's education, so it should also guide our public life. We must stand up resolutely on the international arena for the right to defend ourselves with appropriate information. We should never tie the hands of the defense forces behind their backs because of ineffective foreign policy.

The way we fight against the enemies of the Jewish People must be resolute and uncompromising. One essential component of national defense is deterrence. We should not suffice with defensive action, but we should preempt the enemy and overtake them before they carry out their plots. Also effective retaliation tactics should be used against terrorist attacks. This is the positive side of revenge, which helps us stand erect by showing that our blood is not for sale. Using force can only come through a sense of justice. Indeed, because violence and forcefulness do not come naturally to us as Jews, as long as we are doubtful about our rights to the Land of Israel, we lack the inner justification to fight resolutely against the enemy. This is the root of our current weakness regarding Judea and Samaria, and the very phrase, "occupied territories" belies the simple truth that these are parts of the land that belong to us no less than the pre-'67 borders. Since the attribute of loving-kindness is that which motivates might, our positive relationship of loving the Land of Israel gives us the necessary courage to fight for it.

We must follow the combat morality laid out in the Torah. "The Torah has taught us, 'One who comes to kill you, rise early to kill him first'." This statement could not be truer than when referring to those who attack us, killing and murdering and trying to drive us out of our own country. A complete reassessment must be made of the existing rules of opening fire, which tie the hands of our soldiers behind their backs and endanger their lives. This includes a redefinition of the term "purity of arms" as it is interpreted today in the country. As we know, the gentile nations (even the most enlightened among them) do not follow these standards – which is permitted by international law – yet when it comes to Israel, the nations of the world make impossible demands, expecting us to turn the other cheek.

In conclusion, concessions encourage the enemy. The spiritual power that nurtures the enemy is their hope for achievements, and if our reply to war and terrorism is to speak about giving away land, or even disengage from flourishing Jewish settlements – then with our very own hands, we invite the next terrorist attack, God forbid. Perhaps the most grievous act is releasing murderous terrorists whose hands are full of priceless Jewish blood (referred to ridiculously as "gestures"). This is an unbearable "revolving door" policy whose bitter lesson is written in Jewish blood, yet this nonsense continues. Isn't it clear that these murderers should be punished with the full severity of the law? Isn't it obvious that rewarding their brutality can never lead to true peace? The only thing that can restore Israeli defense policy and return it to its route is by reestablishing it upon its correct basis, which stems from the "Living Torah."

Notes

[1] Genesis 31:42.

[2] *Sanhedrin* 107b.

[3] See, for example: *Ketubot* 26b; Maimonides Laws of Idol Worship 10:6.

[4] Isaiah 2:4.

[5] Isaiah 33:14. See also *Berachot* 60a.

[7]

Step Seven: Jewish Law – Beauty

After the *sefirot* of *chesed* (loving-kindness) and *gevurah* (might) comes the *sefirah* of *tiferet* (beauty), which is attributed to Jacob who is referred to as "The beauty of Israel."[1] Beauty is the ideal blend of loving-kindness and judgments, as harmonious as a magnificent blend of colors. The inner attribute of beauty is compassion – empathizing with another as they are, through conscious choice, respect and attentiveness. While loving-kindness and might correspond to the right and left hands, respectively, beauty corresponds to the torso itself (which is on the central axis of the *sefirot*). This implies that it refers to our innermost identity: the Jewish quality of being "compassionate children of the Compassionate One."[2]

With reference to rectifying the state of Israel, this brings us to Jewish law. In contrast to our present level of beauty, loving-kindness and might are concerned primarily with outward actions; those more physically-manifest aspects of a rectified state. But at the level of beauty we find ourselves asking: By what right can the state truly be called a Jewish state? The root of the word state (מְדִינָה) stems from the concept of judgment (דִין). And the most significant definition of a public sphere is the legal system that runs it.

The current state of affairs – in which rabbinical law courts have limited authority and zero power of law-enforcement, while the state-run law system is founded on a combination of remnants of Ottoman and British law – is in need of an overhaul. The Jewish People have a law system of its own, "And these are the laws that you shall place before them,"[3] covering everything from civil law to criminal law. Obviously, an updated set of statutes and regulations is required to cover all walks of modern life, including business on the stock exchange, or a traffic code – but everything must be under the umbrella of the Torah's laws. Torah law tends neither towards pitiful sensitivity, nor to harsh vengeance. Instead, it is the revelation of the attribute of compassion for all. Indeed, the Zohar equates law with compassion.

In practice, we must remember that as a general rule; Jewish law forbids initiating legal action in court systems that are not committed to Torah law (except in specific cases). We must always make use of the Torah law courts wherever possible, and must set our goal to establish Jewish law in its rightful place in our Jewish state, which is relevant to the judiciary, the legislature and also to the executive branches. Once the legal system is rectified, it will be possible to rejoice in and be proud of the fact that we are citizens of a state that follows the path of justice and honesty, and regard it as the realization of the prophecy, "And I will restore your judges as at first and your counselors as in the beginning; then you shall be called the City of Righteousness, Faithful City. Zion shall be redeemed through justice and her penitent through righteousness."[4]

Notes

1 Lamentations 2:1
2 See *Yevamot* 79a.
3 Exodus 21:1.
4 Isaiah 1:26-27.

[8]

Step Eight: Making Aliyah – Victory

Loving-kindness, might and beauty are the principal attributes of the heart, corresponding to the emotive level of the human psyche. The attributes that follow have a more practical-operative character and represent the lower, more behavioral level of the psyche; like the movement of the legs, which is more powerful than the hands, but less refined. Here, we come to the *sefirah* of *netzach* (victory), corresponding to the right leg, which steps out first.[1] The inner motivating power of the *sefirah* of victory is confidence. This refers to trusting God, which in turn leads to a rectified sense of self-confidence, and the ability to get up and act. The root "victory" (נָצַח) has a number of related connotations: acting resolutely to be victorious and overcome the obstacles that stand in our way; overseeing work and organization (e.g., conducting an orchestra); acting to achieve a stable and long-lasting realization of goals, etc...

In the structure we recommend for rectifying the state, the *sefirah* of victory corresponds to making *aliyah* (immigrating) to Israel, following in the footsteps of Abraham whose first commandment was, "Go for yourself..."[2] The concept of making *aliyah* in the Torah and in our sages' teachings – in contrast to wanderlust and emigration for vague reasons – portrays the sanctity of the Land of Israel and its uniqueness from all other countries. "The Land of Israel is higher than all other countries" and immigrating to the Holy Land is a part of a complete elevation process, "One elevates in sanctity [and does not downgrade]." The pinnacle of ascent is the pilgrimage to the Temple in Jerusalem.

Although the past few generations have seen the immigration of millions of Jews to the Land of Israel, we must not forget that there are millions more who remain in foreign lands, and any Jewish state worthy of its name should encourage *aliyah* as a national goal of the highest priority. How can we encourage *aliyah*? Obviously, the state must open its gates to every Jew, as in the law of return that exists today (which still needs fundamental amendment; see below), by offering benefits and grants to new immigrants (an "absorption basket") and by helping them in the absorption process with substantial assistance. But, the material conditions provided for new immigrants cannot suffice to warm the hearts of our brethren in the Diaspora to immigrate to the Land of Israel. Thank God, *aliyah* these days is considerably quicker and easier than it was during previous generations. However, we should find a way to stimulate the desire to make *aliyah* and warm their hearts to love and live in the Land of Israel, not just as a refuge from persecution, but as an ideal. This goal can be achieved once the country has a pleasing "Jewish face" that will attract every Jew to automatically wish to make his or her home here.

This is why there is a strong connection between rectifying the legal system (which we mentioned with regard to the *sefirah* of beauty) and immigrating to Israel: when the Torah sets the tone of the country, and the sanctity of the land comes to the fore in the public arena – then the natural connection of the Jew to his land will be aroused from its slumber, "Zion shall be redeemed through justice [rectifying the judicial system in the Land of Israel, then] and her returnees through righteousness [referring to the renewed return to Zion]."[3] In addition, mass *aliyah* will result from an amended leadership that strives forward, like that of Moses (who represents the attribute of victory) who brought the Jewish People out of Egypt and led them to the Promised Land.

We should not only teach new immigrants Hebrew in the absorption center, they should also major in how a Jew should behave in the **Holy** Land, in which we are under direct Divine supervision, "A land *Havayah*, your God, looks after; the eyes of *Havayah* your God are always upon it"[4]; living in it demands observing a Torah life according to God's mitzvot with even more care[5]; living in it the Torah and commandments are observed in full;[6] and living in it we will merit heightened spiritual awareness and prophecy. Immigrating to the Land of Israel is infused with a sense of the eternal nature of the Jewish People, "The Eternity of Israel (*netzach yisroel*) does not lie."[7] In essence, this is also true of belief in the Resurrection of the Dead (the eternal nature of every individual Jew), "He gives a soul [Resurrection of the Dead] to the people upon it and spirit to those who walk upon it."[8]

Notes

[1] See *Yoma* 11b; one picks up one's right leg first when walking.

[2] Genesis 12:1.

[3] Isaiah 1:26-27.

[4] Deuteronomy 11:12.

[5] See *Sefer Chassidim* p. 59; *Sefer Shnei Luchot Habrit*, Gate of the Letters, Letter Kuf, The Sanctity of the Land of Israel.

[6] See Nachmanides interpretation on Leviticus 18:25.

[7] I Samuel 15:29.

[8] Isaiah 42:5. See also *Ketubot* 111a, that the Resurrection of the Dead is particularly related to the Land of Israel.

Step Nine: Removing Dangerous Elements – Acknowledgment

Together with the *sefirah* of *netzach* (victory) comes the *sefirah* of *hod* (acknowledgment), as a joint effort of the two legs (also referred to as "two halves of one body"). In the human psyche, the *sefirah* of acknowledgment relates to the ability to be grateful for the good, to admit to sin and to acknowledge the truth, and it is motivated by the quality of sincerity in the soul, "Be sincere with *Havayah* your God."[1] The *sefirah* of victory is relatively "male" and active, while the *sefirah* of acknowledgment is "female" and passive, with a mindset that "everything that God does is for the best."[2] In the psyche, acknowledgment and thanksgiving refine and purify the soul and act like the immune system acts in the body to guard us against unwelcome intrusions to our minds.

With reference to rectifying the state, alongside the positive action of encouraging Jewish immigration, undesirable elements must be prevented from taking hold of the country. Just as the *sefirah* of might accompanies the *sefirah* of loving-kindness and complements it, so too the *sefirah* of acknowledgment accompanies the *sefirah* of victory and guards it from falling into a state of disease [a case of "My glory has turned upon me as a destroyer," where "My glory" (הוֹדִי) is also the possessive form of "acknowledgment" (הוֹד)]. So, for example, although the "Law of Return" is a wonderful idea, nonetheless, we still have an obligation to correct the definition of "Who is a Jew?" since this law currently contains a broad breach through which many gentiles can enter the country (such as 'converts' who did not accept upon themselves to live by the Torah, or hundreds of thousands of Russian immigrants who are not Jewish). So too we cannot ignore the broad phenomenon of illegal foreign immigrants. No civilized country can ever lightheartedly allow a flood of illegal foreign immigrants to drown it, how much more so is this true for a Jewish state, whose main task is to guard its Jewish character by nurturing a sensitivity towards the danger of intermarriage, which for us is an existential question (this in particular will bring great blessing to all of mankind).

At the first phase – as early as possible – we must prevent anyone who endangers our security from residing in the country. This belongs to the earlier stage of the *sefirah* of might, and "Israel's firm arm" by which we deport terrorists (and missionaries, too) who pose an immediate threat to our existence. However, now, in the *sefirah* of acknowledgment, we come to a more comprehensive "root" treatment, which will become possible once the law system has been rectified and follows mass Jewish immigration to the Land of Israel. This treatment relates not only to the obvious enemy but also to the undercover enemy, i.e., any hostile population who pose a long-term security or spiritual danger (such as intermarriage). Therefore emigration for this population to other countries must be encouraged, whether by offering a financial grant, or at least by not offering them with our own hands the optimal conditions necessary to foster a hotbed for terror. Let's recall that when the War of Independence broke out, entire Arab villages fled from the country. However, even if the situation today appears to be different, we must begin repairing our mindset by recognizing our right and our obligation not to leave an antagonistic element in our midst. Indeed, the Torah's warns us, "But if you do not drive out the inhabitants of the Land from before you, then those whom you leave over will be as spikes in your eyes and thorns in your sides, and they will harass you in the land in which you settle."[3]

The general outline for rectification should be based on the description of the three epistles that Joshua sent to the Canaanites who inhabited the Land of Israel before it was conquered by the Children of Israel: "Whoever wishes to flee shall flee. Whoever wishes to make peace shall make peace. Whoever wishes to go to war shall go to war."[4] In this context, we are reminded of Sarah who knew how to demand that Abraham, the man of loving-kindness, should banish Ishmael from their home because he posed a security danger.

At an even more advanced stage, we will be able to apply in full the laws of the "resident foreigner."[5] A resident foreigner is a non-Jew who is committed to observing the seven Noahide laws — the fundamental obligation of every human being.[6] Such residents are entitled to live in the Land of Israel under our auspices and receive select social benefits, as required by the Torah, "A convert or a resident; he shall live with you."[7] However, this can only become possible once the Jewish People is rooted in its land and the law of the Jubilee year is reinstituted, at which stage we will

be capable of incorporating a population of resident for-
eigners without spiritual danger. This stage marks the com-
pletion of the stage of "kingdom" which we discussed in
Step Eleven. However, we cannot allow anyone who
doesn't stand up to the minimal criteria of the resident foreigner to remain in the Land of Israel, just as it would not
be correct to bring home a tenant who has a bad influence
on the family who lives there, "They shall not settle in your
land, lest they bring you to sin against Me."[8]

In Rabbi Shimon's Merit

To conclude, we will mention that Lag Ba'omer corresponds
to "acknowledgment within acknowledgment." In his teachings, Rabbi Shimon bar Yochai (Rashbi) combined the glow-
ing light of the Torah's inner dimension, which opens the
gate to the upper worlds, together with a burning love for
all Jews. Indeed, he was allowed to exit his cave only after
he had learned to love every Jew. From a different perspec-
tive, Rashbi represents an uncompromising assertiveness
towards the enemies of the Jewish People (which was why
he initially had to escape to the cave). This teaches us that
assertiveness against the enemy stems only from pure and
positive incentives, "Lovers of God, hate evil."[9]

Notes

[1] Deuteronomy18:13.
[2] *Berachot* 60b.
[3] Numbers 33:55.
[4] Maimonides, Laws of Kings 6:1-5.

⁵ See Maimonides, Laws of Idolatry, ch. 10; Laws of Forbidden Relations 14:7-8; Laws of Kings, 6:1, 10-11.

⁶ Enumerated in Maimonides Laws of Kings ch. 9.

⁷ Leviticus 25:35; Maimonides Laws of Idolatry 10:2; Nachmanides Reservations on Sefer Hamitzvot, Additional Positive Commandments 17.

⁸ Exodus 23:33.

⁹ Psalms 97:10.

[10]

Step Ten: Education, Torah, Science – Foundation

Following the *sefirah* of *netzach* (victory) on the right and the *sefirah* of *hod* (acknowledgment) on the left, comes the *sefirah* of *yesod* (foundation) in the middle. Foundation centralizes all the *sefirot* above it and is "the seal of truth" – a power that expresses the very essence of the soul with delight and exuberance. The *sefirah* of foundation corresponds to the righteous Joseph – who faithfully guarded his covenant [procreative organ], the limb in the body which corresponds to the *sefirah* of foundation – as the verse states, "And the righteous individual is the foundation of the world."

In the realm of rectifying the state: so far we have been dealing mostly with "politics," including conflicts and wars. But what *really* interests us? What is *really* most important to a Jewish state? Moreover, what exactly do we want a

Jewish state for? Let's hear what our great teacher, Maimonides, has to say about this:[1]

> "The Prophets and the sages did not desire the days of Mashiach so that they could control the world... nor so that they could eat, drink and be merry. Rather, so that they would have respite for the Torah and its wisdom without interruptions or hindrance... and at that time [the time of Mashiach] there will be neither famine nor war, and neither jealously nor competition... and the only quest of the entire world will be to know God... as it says, "For the land will be full of the knowledge of God, like water covers the seabed."[2]

If so, the most important ministry in our state is the Ministry of Education. As of now, and for some time already, we are in a national crisis in the face of a disturbing lack of Jewish education. So, we need to act quickly to promote a Jewish core curriculum: to assure that there is no Jewish boy or girl to whom the fundamental concepts of Judaism are foreign – the prayer book and the synagogue, the Patriarchs and Matriarchs, the Pentateuch and the Prophets, Mishnah, Talmud and Code of Jewish Law, the history of the Jewish People and the great Jewish figures, the Land of Israel and Jerusalem, good virtues and pleasant conduct, Shabbat and kosher food, and so on, with education beginning at infancy and continuing without end. A distinction must be made between principal issues and those that are secondary, and between sacred and secular; therefore, in authentic Jewish education secular studies and vocational training take second place to Torah study, without minimizing the importance of studying a respectful profession.

All this has always been true, but now we are accelerating closer to a spiritual revolution. Until now, Torah and science have usually been perceived as two different fields and sometimes even as conflicting with one another. The Torah is Divine wisdom that descends to us from above, while science is the field of human knowledge which grows out of observing the world around us. However, the complete vision is to unite Torah and science. The Zohar[3] states that the world is destined for a flood of knowledge (like water covers the seabed). And just as the flood in the days of Noah occurred as the result of "All the springs of the great deep were split, and the windows of the heavens opened up,"[4] in the same way, the flood of wisdom will come from two complementary sources: human wisdom, as "the springs of the great deep [which burst open from below]" and the Torah, as "the windows of the heavens opened up [from above]." Science will substantiate the Torah for all to see, and the Torah will illuminate and enrich science with a new light.

Select individuals throughout the ages have dealt with this task – such as the righteous Joseph, who was a phenomenal sage both in worldly wisdom and Divine knowledge. Currently a "Torah Academy" should be established in which students study "secular studies in pure sanctity." However, the ultimate relationship between the two will manifest through the full revelation of Divine Providence, as stated with reference to Mashiach in whose days will be revealed, "A new Torah,"[5] meaning that new, more profound facets of the Torah that Moses transmitted to us will be revealed.

Notes

1 Laws of Kings 12:4.
2 Isaiah 11:9.
3 Zohar I, 116b.
4 Genesis 7:11.
5 *Vayikra Rabah* 13:3.

[11]

Step Eleven: Towards the Kingdom of Israel – Kingdom

The final *sefirah* is *malchut* (kingdom), the ability for rectified self-expression in speech and action, by recognizing that I am a vessel that receives all energy from above, with nothing that I call my own, "For from You is everything and from Your Hand we have given it to You."[1] The inner power of kingdom is positive lowliness – the attribute of King David, who said, "And I am lowly in my eyes."[2] It is specifically this power that gives us the ability to rise up and rule without a trace of negative arrogance.

In the public realm, we must remember that the goal of a Jewish state is to become the Kingdom of Israel. When we recall all that the evil kings of the past had in mind for the Jewish People and for all of humankind, our natural instinct is to recoil from the concept of a monarchy. However, the desired Jewish King is the complete opposite of a tyrannical dictator, as Maimonides[3] describes, "In the way that Scriptures paid great respect [to the king]... so too they commanded that his heart should be lowly and hollow inside him, as it states, 'and my heart is hollow within me,'[4] and he should not act too harshly with the Jewish People, as it states, 'so that his heart shall not be elevated above his brethren,'[5] and he should be gracious and merciful to the small and the great, involving himself in their care and wellbeing. He should protect the honor of even the humblest of men... He should always conduct himself with great humility... a king is referred to as a shepherd... as the Prophets have described the behavior of a shepherd, 'He shall pasture His flock like a shepherd, He shall gather the lambs with His arm and carry them at His chest.'[6]"

Also to be remembered is that the Sanhedrin is at the king's side, with broad jurisdiction powers. It is also possible that together with the king a controlling establishment – a government elected by the people – may continue to be involved in the ongoing management of the country.[7] Nonetheless, the king is the one who leads us toward great destinations, such as building the Temple, and his very existence is a bridge that arouses honor to accepting the Kingdom of Heaven. This is how the sages interpret the double expression, "You shall surely appoint [lit.: appoint you shall appoint] a king upon you."[8] "'Appoint' – God's Kingdom; 'you shall appoint' – a flesh and blood king as mentioned with reference to King Solomon, 'and Solomon sat upon God's throne as king.'[9]"

On the one hand, the commandment to appoint a king is a commandment given to us, "The Jewish People were commanded three commandments as they entered the Land [the first of which is] to appoint a king, as it says, 'You shall surely appoint a king upon you.'" Yet, on the other hand, the verse is referring to a Divine goal and promise [i.e., to be revealed from above, not appointed from below], "The

Mashiach will stand in the future and return the kingdom of David to the former glory of the first government, and he will build the Temple, and gather in distant Jews. All of the laws will return in his days, as they previously were: the sacrifices will be offered, and Sabbatical and Jubilee years will be kept according to all the commandments that are in the Torah."[10] But, how will Mashiach come? The sages have already offered two possibilities: either miraculously or naturally.[11] In either case, we are not exempt from acting to reinstate the Kingdom of Israel in a practical way, and it might be that out of our actions come success, thus indicating Divine acceptance. Once this king is appointed, we may then realize that this king is Mashiach according to Maimonides qualifications, "If he acted and was successful and built the Temple in its place and gathered in the distant Jews, then this is definitely Mashiach."[12]

On the one hand, we talk about a monarchy as a final goal, and even if he tarries we will wait for him. Yet, on the other hand, even now it is possible to derive a practical approach from the commandment to appoint a king, and it is our duty to work toward a rectified leadership. And if the process is accelerated, and Mashiach comes today – we will welcome him warmly!

Notes

[1] I Chronicles 29:14.
[2] II Samuel 6:22.
[3] Laws of Kings 2:6.
[4] Psalms 109:22.

[5] Deuteronomy 17:20.

[6] Isaiah 40:11.

[7] Such as the power of the "City's Good Ones" in Jewish law.

[8] Deuteronomy 17:15.

[9] I Chronicles 29:23; see also, *Derech Mitzvoteicha*, the commandment to appoint a king.

[10] Maimonides Laws of Kings 1:1.

[11] *Sanhedrin* 98a; see also *Or Hachayim*, Numbers 24:17.

[12] Laws of Kings 11:4.

About the Author

Rabbi Yitzchak Ginsburgh is one of our generation's fore-most expositors of Kabbalah and Chassidut and is the au-thor of over 100 books in Hebrew and English (which have also been translated into French, Russian, Spanish, and Por-tuguese). He is known for his breakthrough insights into the interface between Torah and science, and his teachings have revolutionized Jewish thought on this subject. He is also the founder and dean of the Ba'al Shem Tov School of Jewish Psychology, and his unique approach to mathemat-ics in Torah is now the basis of a new math curriculum for Jewish schools. For more of Rabbi Ginsburgh's teachings, please visit Inner.org.

www.ingramcontent.com/pod-product-compliance
Lightning Source LLC
Chambersburg PA
CBHW021146020426
42331CB00005B/926